Watch & Learn

Designing, writing, commissioning &
producing effective video drama for learning

Tom Hickmore

Cover image by: Nice Media
Book design by: SWATT Books Ltd

Printed in the United Kingdom
First Printing, 2021

ISBN: 978-1-7399300-0-4 (Hardback)
ISBN: 978-1-7399300-1-1 (eBook)

Nice Media Limited
Brighton, East Sussex
BN1 4GW

www.nicemedia.co.uk

For Humphrey and Louis.
Never stop learning.

WATCH & LEARN

Contents

Introduction

Drama in L&D faces three main challenges – low budgets, low expectations, and sparse knowledge of the medium. This book brings knowledge, which in turn raises expectations of what is possible. With a following wind, this can mean improved quality, leading to evidenced success which might even attract more budget.

It was way back in the 1980's when I first got into making corporate video. Quite quickly I found myself very much enjoying drama, but I didn't fancy working in TV. Coming from a video art background, I liked the craft feel of making smaller productions with greater control. So, in the '90's I focused on directing and producing interactive drama for learning. In those days the distribution was on CD-ROM and the video playback images were tiny, the size of... mobile phone screens – smaller actually. I enjoyed making content that has a real-world effect, content that's going to help someone in a practical way.

© Julie Edwards

Wherever you are in the L&D world, you'll know the way to achieve a lot with a modest budget is good design. By which I mean considerations like the best creative approach to take given the learning objectives, the nature of the content, audience expectations and crucially, and this is where this book earns its corn, making best use of the budget!

In this book I distil some high-level knowledge from everything I've learned about drama in learning over 30-plus years to give you the key tools to design and write your own drama projects.

This book should also be of interest to anyone commissioning drama, to help them understand what it's good for and how it works. It's intended to be entirely practical in the hope that, for you the reader, "practice" will, as they say, "make perfect"!

My chapters are in a logical order if you are keen to drink in the whole thing, but to accommodate those who'd rather skip through to the bits they most need I've included a summary of learning points at the end of each chapter.

I believe drama to be one of the best tools to enable behaviour change. Join me on a mission to improve the standard of drama produced in our sector!

1.

What is drama?

"I want to elevate the mundane".

- Pamela Adlon

In the corporate training world, "drama" is often lumped together with workplace role-play scenarios performed by staff and simulations or "sims" – which are role-plays by actors.

Both forms involve people acting, but there the similarity to drama ends. A role-play is a demonstration of an interaction whereas a drama, while it may sometimes have a similar appearance, works on a more complex set of principles.

Drama comprises an array of techniques that allow us to model human behaviour. Using characters, drama models the world views of others, allowing us to step into their shoes. By populating a landscape with these modelled entities, we shed light upon the issues they embody and upon which they gaze.

© Nice Media

Let's remind ourselves of the power of filmed drama. People dedicate their lives to the pursuit and worship of movie stars. When we want to feel smart, we quote famous lines from movies. We want to live in movies. We visit theme parks and dress up as our favourite characters. There's endless social media chat about what has happened and what is about to happen in TV drama. All this is not because film drama presents wild, escapist fantasies, but because, in the movies, the world is ordered, actions have consequences, and everything makes sense. That is what films do for us. *They allow the world to make sense.*

The strongest use of drama in learning is to help your audience make sense of things. Strangely, the way to do that is to take them to a *new world.*

©Nice Media

At home and at work, we are different people. Workplace culture is formed around mutually agreed rules for how to manage our private selves within the organisation. This Venn diagram overlap delineates the world in which our stories take place. It's the spot where public overlaps private. It's a version of the world we can all buy into because, while we all manage it in our own way, we can all identify it as something that needs to be managed.

How do we get along with people we may not choose as friends? How do we cope with the unruly feelings that difficult work situations can give rise to? Drama provides a safe space in which to reflect upon these challenges.

Learning Points

- Drama is distinct from role-play.

- Drama consists of an array of techniques that allow us to model human behaviour.

- Drama and movies show us a world in which things make sense.

- Drama for the workplace concerns that space where public overlaps private. It's about how we manage our emotions and get along at work.

2.
The role of drama in workplace learning

"Good directors don't answer questions with their work. They generate debate and create discussion."

- Alejandro Gonzalez Inarritu

Danny is one of the senior members of the sales team. He's been in this job for ages! He can do it with his eyes shut. Sometimes he bends the rules. Because, after all these years, he knows an important rule from a trivial one.

© Nice Media

Audrey, his younger colleague, has only just learned the rules. She was a keen student. But, coming up against Danny, her compliance is tested and tested, until one day she goes along with Dan's rule-bending a bit too much and they lose a client. Compliance training is mostly useless. It's literal box-ticking until the culture that brings about non-compliance is challenged.

© Nice Media

Oliver is a guy with a problem. He works in accounts where one of his colleagues, he feels, treats him differently from his co-workers, who are white. He can't talk about it. It's difficult. This issue can be brought out in a corporate story - enacted and shared so we can all see that unconscious bias is real and discussion of the topic is made easier.

© Nice Media

Pete can get very angry at work. He sees a lot of painful things in the world of adult safeguarding. How can Pete handle his feelings when dealing with colleagues in other agencies with overlapping responsibilities? Agencies that he feels have made mistakes. What's going on in his head is probably a bit scary – mixed up with the emotions he experiences in his case work.

© Nice Media

Through drama, Pete, and others like him, can share some of their vulnerabilities. And the people who have to work with him, get to feel okay discussing this edgy stuff in a safe space.

Anthropologist Robin Dunbar observed a correlation between the size of a primate's brain and the average size of its social group. He reckons humans have evolved to live in groups of around 150. As society expanded, we therefore needed to evolve laws and enforce norms to maintain stability and cohesion in a larger society. Storytelling is a tool from this box. It's the device that allows us to manage enormous groups of people as if they were small villages.

The use of drama in the corporate world is, therefore, clear. It can tell powerful stories, but it is no good for teaching the fussy details of a subject. Drama can deliver deep and important messages with emotional impact. A successful learning drama is one that is deep rather than wide. That core message may be all you need to deliver or, if you position detailed learning strategically around it, drama can carry people through a learning journey.

If a learner can relate to the meaning and purpose of what they are doing, they will be more inclined and better able to apply themself to the elements of study that take time and self-discipline. To put it another way, and this is aligned to research, we only think deeply about the things we care about.

Although watching a video drama is the most relaxing and effortless type of learning, it is only successful if we manage to get the viewer to do some work. Drama poses human problems and asks us to solve them. What would you do in that situation? Imagining yourself in the situation - that is the active part. And drama is especially sneaky at making us active in a way that uses our deepest imagination. That's an amazing power that can directly affect behaviour. So how shall we go about it? A little bit of film theory can shed a lot of light on how best to design drama for learning.

Learning Points

- Drama in the workplace is a powerful way to stimulate discussion about difficult subjects.

- Anthropology suggests that storytelling is an evolved tool to manage large groups.

- Drama brings meaning, and meaning means motivation.

- Watching a drama seems passive, but it's only successful if the audience's imagination is active.

3.

Dialectical Storytelling

"Let the cut tell the story. Otherwise you have not got dramatic action, you've got narration."

– David Mamet

Many of the mechanisms in drama are dialectical. Thesis, antithesis to synthesis. You tell a story with a series of conflicting events. First, we see *this* - revealing one idea, then we see *that* – revealing a second idea. We race to a conclusion, which is dashed by the next idea we are presented with. This is a dialectical viewing experience. It's the structure within a scene and between scenes.

When actors talk, they are not exchanging information – they are exchanging blows. Drama is driven by conflict and the actors are active, not passive. A guiding principle to creating a suite of characters is that there should be innate conflict, that's how the story is generated. A dramatic storyline is a series of worldview conflicts, with each step of the conflict shedding new light on the issue the characters are fighting over.

A director tells a story with a series of ideas. A film isn't lines of speech cut together; it's a series of ideas cut together. A facial expression or an action communicates an idea as well as a line of dialogue. Idea one is knocked by idea two, which suggests a third idea in the head of the viewer. It's a dialectic.

The early Soviet filmmaker, Lev Kuleshov, proved this principle with a famous experiment. He cut together short, silent film sequences in which he got Tsarist matinee idol Ivan Mosjoukine to perform a completely neutral expression looking direct to-camera. He cut this in a sequence next to an image of a girl in a coffin. Audiences were shown the sequence and asked to report the emotion on his face. They invariably interpreted it as sadness. Kuleshov then repeated the experiment inserting different cutaway shots, such as a bowl of soup and a beautiful woman reclining. In each case, audiences responded by projecting their assumptions about what a character might be feeling in that situation – hunger or sexual arousal - onto the face of the actor. The dialectic in action.

Of course, we are rarely aware of these mechanisms at work within us. When we recount watching a drama, in our minds it felt like we were watching people talking.

But drama isn't watching people talking; it's watching people in conflict. Actors aren't playing the dialogue and directors aren't directing the talking (the text), the substance is in the subtext. Subtext is what happens emotionally in a scene and is often, and most compellingly, at odds with what is being said.

Film direction suffered with the introduction of sound to film, because one could get away with allowing dialogue to tell the story. But, this is just explaining what's happening, rather than showing it happening. Explanation is neither dramatic nor engaging.

So, the dialectic is the first principle of drama.

This might be a good moment to share an idea from Alfred Hitchcock. He often spoke of the difference between surprise and suspense. Suppose we show a scene of two people talking and suddenly a bomb explodes and they are both killed. This is a surprise. It gets your attention, but not necessarily in a good way. Now, suppose we do a re-run of the scene, but letting the audience know there is a ticking time bomb under the table during the discussion. Now, every line, every word becomes laden with new meaning. Our attention is held.

Learning Points

- The dialectic – idea conflicting with idea to produce a third idea in your head – is fundamental to drama.

- Soviet filmmaker Lev Kuleshov proved that we read meaning into simple juxtaposition of imagery.

- Drama produces meaning by showing conflict between characters.

- A scene is less about the dialogue than it is about the conflict that lays beneath the text.

4.

Character

Does a story begin with an event or a character? A story is about a character, so the two are inseparable. It's like that well-known tree falling in a forest. The event has not occurred unless someone is there to witness it.

© Tom Hickmore

A character exists to bring meaning to your subject matter. You are writing a story about how *that character* interacts with the subject matter. This chapter is about designing characters.

Learning designers, untrained in dramatic technique, too often put the camera in the position of the protagonist, believing that this will create empathy and, while they're at it, rather neatly dodge the problem of the representation of diversity. There are some occasions in which a literal point-of-view may be appropriate, but it is a poor solution to these problems. The good news is – the tools in this book will allow you to come up with far better solutions.

What's amazing about the way drama works is that a character can be as unwholesome as you like, and we can still empathise with them. You don't have to share a character's moral outlook to understand why they act as they do. Drama is a powerful way to immerse yourself in another's point of view.

Drama is naturally inclusive because what a character wears, their body mass index or the colour of their skin has little impact on how we relate to them. Neither do other aspects of external characterization, like how polite they are, their hobbies or personal habits, stand in the way of our ability to empathise with them. In fact, flaws are the most potent and attractive elements in our palette. Think of all the movie characters you've rooted for, but would never think of having as a house guest:

© AA Film Archive / Alamy Stock Photo

The Terminator – a soulless robot assassin; Robin Hood - the left-wing vigilante; Gordon Gekko - the unprincipled, charming corporate raider and hero of Wall Street; Buffy the Vampire Slayer – a cheerleader with a thing about dead guys.

PictureLux / The Hollywood Archive / Alamy Stock Photo

The principal way to make a character sympathetic is to give them motivation. Think of Walter White, the protagonist of Breaking Bad. The character is a nerdy, irritable, not particularly attractive, chemistry teacher of 50. But we learn he has a younger wife, a disabled son and another child on the way. To support them he works extra hours at a car wash, (where his pupils come to laugh at him). But the pressure is too much, he collapses and is rushed to hospital. There he receives a diagnosis of terminal lung cancer. That's all the motivation the viewer needs to be able to understand why this everyday guy gets into the illegal narcotics business.

I can't emphasise this enough - you need characters who are flawed and make mistakes, not simply because they are interesting but because you want characters who create conflict, or else you have no story. Naturally, large organisations have a fear of representing their staff as anything less than perfect. The answer is to show us the motivation. It's as simple as that. A person at work might cut corners and not follow the rules if they are stressed. Show us the reason for their stress. Make it part of your story.

Fictional characters, of course, aren't people, they are concise creations that seem like people. They are a device to communicate. In L&D I sometimes feel that because we are writing about ordinary people we know, we are inhibited in depicting their inner struggles. Yes, there are limits to propriety, but equally we do our audience and the medium a disservice if we merely draw superficial characters. In fact, the deeper you go with a character, and the more you explore their flaws, paradoxically, the more people will perceive your film as a comfortable fiction, while simultaneously being more likely moved by it.

In all forms of perception, our minds fill in gaps from scanty information with assumptions. This mechanism is negatively bound up with the stereotyping of people, but we can use it to our advantage with archetypes. We all embody different archetypes in different situations. Sometimes I might be a lost child, and at other times a bossy husband. These kinds of archetype are how we think of members of our family: the clumsy one, mum's favourite, the controlling older sister. When creating characters, we use such archetypal elements to communicate quickly and efficiently.

The key dramatic archetypes are defined by their role in the narrative. There's the protagonist, of which the hero is a variety. Then there's the baddy, the antagonist – the character who seeks the same goal as the protagonist, but who's motivation is morally wrong. These two characters are the engine of most stories, with the supporting characters reflecting and articulating aspects of them.

Protagonist vs antagonist = conflict = story. Batman versus the Joker, Ripley vs the Alien, Clarice Starling vs Hannibal Lecter.

The antagonist can also be non-human, like a mountain that needs to be climbed, an organization (e.g. the Mafia), or an ideology (such as the Patriarchy). But even these things must be characterized according to the story you want to tell. The indomitable mountain that has defeated so many brave climbers; the Mafia - a club for dysfunctional mummy's boys; the Patriarchy – the life force of a million chauvinistic men given independent agency, it is blind and seductive and grinds you down.

There are many schools of narrative, each of which lays out its own set of archetypes. Rather like the Roman's view of local gods, we can see that the Jupiter of one civilization is the Zeus of another.

Here are 8 useful character archetypes.

PROTAGONIST: The story is about this character. They drive the action. We root for them and want them to succeed. The notion of a protagonist comes from ancient Greek drama, where the term originally meant, "the player of the first part or the chief actor" and, incidentally, where hero meant "demigod".

ANTAGONIST: Opposes the protagonist. They represent the problem that must be overcome. They want the same thing as the protagonist, but seek to achieve it by other means.

REASON: This character makes all their decisions based on logic, never letting their feelings get in the way.

EMOTION: Emotion has no filter – they are always acting on their feelings and ignoring the rational inconveniences of their decisions.

SCEPTIC: Something of a depressive nerd. They expect the worst, which can be a curse, until their rational pessimism turns out to be right, and then they are invaluable.

SIDEKICK: Like a cheerleader who cheers from the side-lines. Usually close to the protagonist, they may also be attached to the antagonist.

GUARDIAN: The Guardian, also described as Mentor, is a teacher and helper to the protagonist. As Conscience she can be a moral guide for the audience.

CONTAGONIST: The Contagonist hinders and deludes the protagonist, tempting her to take the wrong course or approach.

You'll recognise many of these from popular TV and film.

In our very human, leaping-to-conclusions-about-people way, an audience getting a sniff of an archetype in a character will at once pigeonhole them and assume they have a range of traits associated with that archetype. This provides you with an opportunity to play with those expectations. As Hollywood screenwriter William Goldman said: "Give the reader what they want, just not the way they expect it."

So, as we develop a character and recognise their similarity to an archetype, we can then beef up some of those archetypal elements, or constructively confound them.

A character can combine more than one archetype, as is often the case in stories with a small cast. And characters can defy the habits of their archetypes. After all, this is fiction.

Characterization provides the superficial aspects of a character, (mannerisms, accent, clothes), while deep character is defined by their actions in the story. We understand a character by observing their actions. Will they do the right thing when the pressure mounts? Stories hinge on moral choices, by which they create meaning.

Character building technique

Here's a technique for creating convincing characters. Use positive and negative character facets to build depth. Often, such positive and negative traits can be two sides of the same coin. Here's a list:

POSITIVE	NEGATIVE
Confident	Arrogant
Shy	Thoughtful
Visionary	Narcissistic
Fundamentalist	Rule-abiding
Optimistic	Self-deluded
Neurotic	Perceptive
Detail-oriented	Can't see the bigger picture
Inspired	Lazy
Dictatorial	Gets things done
Loyal	Passive-aggressive
Pleasing	Deferential
Genius	Anti-social
Forgiving	Flaky
Benevolent	Low self-esteem

I dreamed up an antagonist who is a Bad Boss. Here's a table of elements brought together to describe her.

© Nice Media

BAD BOSS CHARACTER MATRIX	
FUNCTION	Antagonist
NAME	Theresa
GENDER	Female
JOB ROLE	Managing director
AGE	Late 30's
POSITIVE CHARACTER FACET	Visionary
NEGATIVE CHARACTER FACET	Narcissist
EXTERNAL CHARACTERISATION	Upper class hipster
Flaw - her vision doesn't match up to reality.	

Of course, rules can be broken. The thing to know is that breaking the rules has consequences. If you have a passive protagonist, you tend to get a story of despair. In the standard approach, the protagonist is active and is driven to change things. A story like that, even if it doesn't have a happy ending, gives us a feeling of agency and meaning.

People who write novels and feature films often imagine deep and detailed lives for their characters — stretching right back to their birth and childhood. It is unlikely we need to go to those lengths in our characterisations.

The character development we have done, however, must be defined in a short form that works for the cast, director and production team. I don't know of a standard format for this, but the character sheet below serves well.

The first example is a profile for Don Draper, the lead in the TV drama Mad Men.

© PictureLux / The Hollywood Archive / Alamy Stock Photo

CHARACTER	Don Draper, Lead
WHO defining attributes	Ad Executive / Alcoholic / Imposter
WHAT actions past, present and future	War vet / Stolen identity / Closes huge deals / Cheats on wife
WHERE physical settings	Downtown NY Office / Client Offices / High-end Bars and Lounges / Suburban Home
WANTS character desires	Privacy / Freedom / Power
SUMMARY character breakdown	Meet Don, he's an ad executive based in Manhattan during the 1960's. Don appears to be an average family man, but he's got a secret. He's actually an alcoholic, adulterer, and his real name isn't even Don Draper! He stole someone's identity years ago and has been posing as them. How can Don hide all this? He's that good at his job. When Don sells you something, you buy it. But recently, his world has started falling apart.
COSTUME NOTES	Always impeccably dapper – usually in a tailored lounge suit.

And now a profile of a character in an office-based learning drama:

WATCH & LEARN

CHARACTER	Susan
WHO defining attributes	Project manager / Partner in consultancy / Self-defines as scrupulously fair
WHAT actions past, present and future	Publishing background / Been at Tortwell for 10 years / Her mentoring of Holly becomes favouritism
WHERE physical settings	Office / Meeting Room / Coffee lounge
WANTS character desires	Success / Respect / Conflict-free team
SUMMARY character breakdown	Susan is a hard-working, intelligent and successful project manager. She's experienced, focused, confident and energized. Process not people focused. Not naturally empathetic but tries to be fair. Scots.
COSTUME NOTES	Smart. Conservative dresser.

Equally, you can present this type of information in prose form.

Anyone who writes drama develops their own techniques and tools, and there are plenty you can find online. I've shared some of the more straightforward ones. The main thing to know about writing character is that an actor and director really need to know what's going on under the bonnet. And if you don't write it for them, they'll very likely make it up.

Learning Points

- In a drama, events are meaningless until a character reacts to them.

- A character's function is to bring meaning to your subject matter.

- Characterization is about superficial elements of a character, whereas deep character is defined by actions in a story – how they respond to moral challenge.

- Drama allows us to empathise with any type of character – good or bad, of any race, shape or size.

- We naturally assign people to archetypes based on the slimmest of clues. This can be used to the advantage of the dramatist.

- Most drama is built on the conflict between protagonist and antagonist.

- If you only write very superficial characters, the director and actors will make up their own deeper aspects of the characters.

5.

Story

"A story should have a beginning, a middle, and an end... but not necessarily in that order."

– Jean-Luc Godard

Storytelling is a device that has evolved alongside the development of larger, complex social structures – allowing us to manage an enormous company of people as if it were a small village. Stories communicate emotionally when information and instruction aren't enough. Stories are not about information, they are about a deeper message. This is a good thing to do, this is bad. Stories are about morality.

© Marcos Oliveira

Who is our story about? Someone who understands and acts within the morality of our subject matter. The story tests the moral boundaries of our subject area. A story about diversity must explore the strange injustices in unexpected ways. Depicting a clear case of racial prejudice will likely come across as a lecture. Make your story about a grey area – a dispute in which we don't know who is guilty – and you'll be speaking on a level to your audience. Invite them to join you in a moral exploration. The aim is to get the audience actively engaged - thinking for themselves. And if we do it well, we can stimulate discussion around the issue.

Stories need conflict. A protagonist seeks something, but someone or something is stopping her from getting it. Stories are about learning through struggle.

Beginning, middle and end. This is the simplest paradigm of a story. Three acts:

- Set-up
- Confrontation
- Resolution

Within this structure lay the events:

- Inciting Incident
- Progressive Complications
- Crisis
- Climax
- Resolution

Here's a diagram:

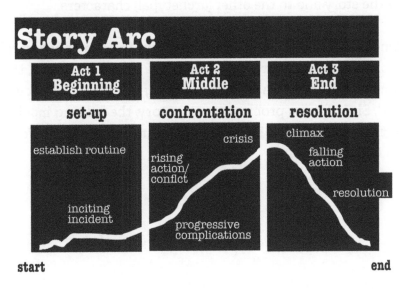

Diagram: Jonathan Swain

Act 1 - The Set-up

In the set-up we reveal who the characters are and what is important to them. We introduce the protagonist, state the dramatic premise (what the story is about) and reveal the dramatic situation.

Such contextual exposition is an essential component of a story, but explaining the context of a story is not dramatic. We, therefore, seek to reduce exposition to a minimum and to dramatize what remains. For more information on how to dramatize exposition see chapter 6 on "Text".

In corporate learning we can often explain the context of the story outside the video – some text in a course for example. We can also take shortcuts - giving a character a job role that will immediately give her a known relationship to the subject of the story and to the other (archetypal) characters.

Once we have established the normality of our imagined world, along comes a disturbance. This is the inciting incident, that kicks off the story. In Jaws, the inciting incident is "shark eats girl, Sheriff has a problem". In Toy Story, the inciting incident is the arrival of Buzz Lightyear, threatening to displace Woody as Andy's favourite.

Corporate drama inciting incidents might be: an emergency call handler receives a call from an old man who has fallen and may have broken a limb; or a protagonist notices a colleague bending the rules and thus putting their team at risk.

Act 2 – The Confrontation

In the second act, the protagonist sets out to rectify what's gone wrong in her world. But every time she takes an action the world does not respond as she expected. Instead, the problem worsens, and the stakes get higher. These are progressive complications.

In the story first mentioned in chapter two, the protagonist, Audrey, noticed a colleague, Danny, bending the rules, endangering himself, the team and the organisation. Now she has a word with him. Nevertheless, Danny's behaviour worsens. He may have an addiction of some kind. Every time she tries to help him, he lets her down and she becomes gradually more complicit. The stakes are raised as the personal risk of blowback gets unbearable.

All these progressive complications lead inevitably to a crisis. The crisis is when the protagonist MUST make a choice under pressure. Ideally the crisis decision should be a dilemma – a choice between two evils. An impossible choice. The harder the choice, the more engaging it is for the viewer, and the more it will shed light on your moral message. Should Audrey report Danny with the inevitable repercussions on him and the guilt she will feel? Or should she just cut herself off from him, transferring to another team and giving up everything she has invested here?

"Confronted by an ultimate dilemma and face to face with the most powerful antagonistic forces, the protagonist must choose one action or another in a last attempt to gain the object of desire" wrote the great screenwriting guru Robert McKee.

This is a heart-stopping crisis moment, in which we get a peek into the protagonist's soul, while we contemplate her deepest dilemma, she now makes her choice and events tumble out from that decision.

© Nice Media

As the decision is made, we are tipped into Act 3.

Act 3 – The Resolution

In our story Audrey, the protagonist, shows character by choosing a third way. She persuades Danny to get help.

The climax shows the consequences of the decision played out. Witnessing a moral action into which we have a human insight gives us a meaningful experience. This is the peak moment for the creation of meaning in the minds of our audience.

The story is now told, but we still have our audience's attention, and they want to know what happens next. The audience enjoy seeing the consequences of the moral choice played out in a resolution. How has the resonating force of the climax changed the world for others? Danny speaks to management and is given help – a satisfying result. But it would still be satisfying if Audrey had reported Danny and he had resigned, bitter. An unhappy ending perhaps. Our satisfaction is derived from the generation of meaning as we watch what are, without our interpretation, meaningless events.

While this structure can be found in most stories, we can, of course, mess with it. If we choose to have no moral resolution – no consequence from the moral action – we will produce a story that is disturbing or sad. If we have no discernible story line – we've got an existentialist drama which reminds us that events and our lives have no meaning.

Many learning dramas are fractions of a story. The better you understand which part of a larger story you are offering to your audience, the more resonant you can make it.

Learning Points

- Storytelling is an evolved tool for managing large groups.

- Stories deliver morality.

- The 3-act structure describes a classic design for a story.

- It consists of inciting incident, progressive complications, crisis, climax and resolution.

- The crisis is when the protagonist is faced by a thematic dilemma.

- The climax is when the protagonist's choice, in the face of the dilemma, is revealed.

- This moment of choice is the moment of maximum generation of meaning for the viewer.

6.

Text

"When the screenplay has been written and the
dialogue has been added, we're ready to shoot"

- Alfred Hitchcock

Part 1: Dialogue

Suppose you have to write some dialogue tomorrow – what do
you need to know?

1. If you can possibly get away with not writing any, do so!
    Watch a good film with the sound down and you pretty
    much know what's going on. It's a visual medium, with
    most of the audience's attention going to the image.

© Nice Media

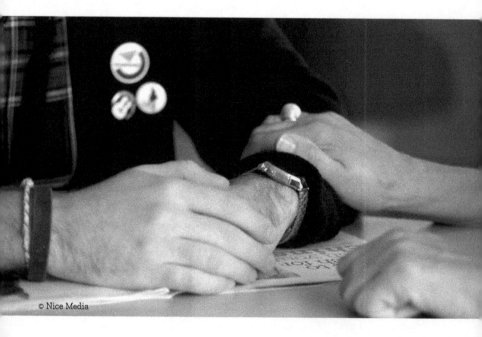
© Nice Media

WATCH & LEARN

2. Dialogue is messy. If you pay attention to the conversation around you, you will notice it's chaotic and ungrammatical, with mumbled words, slang and incomplete sentences. Dramatic dialogue must maintain this everyday feel while doing a lot of story work. Each line pushes the narrative forward a notch, bouncing between characters as the ideas of the story are tested and developed.

3. People don't say what they mean. Two old friends chatting about the weather are really saying how much they like to spend time together. This emotional layer of meaning in a scene is its subtext. The more polarized the text and subtext the more interesting the dialogue. A couple splitting up – expressing it in polite terminology. There's plenty of scope for this in a corporate environment, because the story is always about duty, and the emotional difficulties we have with that duty form the subtext.

4. People don't say what they would like to say. Even when people are desperate to communicate something important, they're seldom direct. Asking someone to marry you, you might talk all around the subject before you dared pop the question. Firing someone – you wouldn't say "You're fired!" you'd lead up to it gradually and then use a euphemism. Text and subtext are at odds. Indirectness is both realistic and dramatic.

5. Dialogue doesn't sound nice. The moment you congratulate yourself on a well-turned phrase it's a good sign that you should probably cut that line. The best art doesn't draw attention to itself.

6. Write in short exchanges of speech. The joy of dialogue is the rapid exchange between individuals. It's a football match not keepie-uppie. Meaning is built as the narrative flows through a series of "world-view filters" (characters). If you do need to write a monologue, break it up with the reactions of other characters and reactions by the speaker to what they are saying: "She pauses, realizing the significance of what she just said."

7. Read it aloud. When you've written dialogue, read it out loud to see what you stumble upon. There is a physical aspect to dialogue that must be acknowledged.

8. Use suspense structure. To keep audience attention, write the suspense sentence. Keep the audience hanging on every word. Leave the object of the sentence until the end.

Not:

> AUDREY
> I'm going to report you, I've got no choice - I'm so sorry Danny.

Rather:

> AUDREY
> I'm so sorry Danny, I've got no choice - I'm going to report you.

This same notion of suspense, of not revealing any more of the situation than is necessary to keep attention, is the design principle for every speech, every scene and the entire piece.

9. Use different voices. Take care to give your characters distinctive voices – their own unique turns of phrase.

10. Don't put the learning into the mouths of the characters. If a character becomes a mouthpiece for the learning, they will immediately lose credibility with the audience – unless they are characterized as a separated commentator. The meaning of the learning is in the events depicted, not in the dialogue.

11. Dramatize exposition. Take that story from the last chapter:

> AUDREY
> Look Danny, I've covered for you
> for six months now, and you keep
> letting me down, cutting corners
> and endangering the team.

It achieves its plot work very well – communicating all the salient points of exposition for us to understand the exchange that will follow. But audiences know that people rarely speak in a way that conveniently updates someone who happens to be listening in. The artifice is apparent.

So, let's ask ourselves, how would our protagonist be feeling? Let's imagine, in our wider work to develop

Audrey's character, we've learned her mother was an alcoholic, so she ended up chief carer for her brother. Thus she has a parental attitude to Danny, even though he's older than her. This information can be backstory and need not to be revealed to the audience, but it gives depth to our character. The knowledge of this situation informs how we can shape this dialogue.

```
                    AUDREY
        Come  on  Danny,  when  are  you
        going  to  sort  yourself  out?
        It's been six months now.
```

It's not much of a change, but already it seems more natural. A tiny change has brought emotional tension and character insight.

Screenwriting guru Robert McKee urges us to "turn exposition into ammunition." Take expositional information and make drama out of it. Make it mean something to your characters and it can become the subject of a dispute.

© United Archives GmbH / Alamy Stock Photo

The James Bond movies always have an exposition problem as they need to explain what all the gadgets do. It's solved by making the gadget exposition scene into a character duel. Schoolboy show-off Bond is patronized cruelly by toff prof Q. (Note the archetypes). The conflict makes the exchange of information dramatic, giving us entertaining insight into the characters and we forgive or forget its transparently expositional nature.

Let's look at a workplace example. To make head or tail of a scene about managing a case of bullying in the workplace it's desirable for our manager protagonist, and our audience, to understand the salient details of the case. But if we begin with the victim revealing all, it won't seem convincing, and we've missed out the first beat of our drama. The manager teases the facts from the victim, who, because of his inner turmoil, is in denial about the situation. Now this is a scene of conflict.

Ever seen a learning drama like this?

FRED
So this must be the new seven-fifty. I believe it can print five hundred pages a minute and has a lifetime warranty.

LILY
Yes, great isn't it? Not only that, but it remembers my log-in code and asks me if I want to repeat my favourite tasks. Saves a lot of time.

This is exposition that is not dramatized, but rather shoved it into the mouths of characters. What I call "ideas on sticks."

By developing these character profiles and motivations, the dialogue will rewrite itself. If we model Fred as a manager obsessed with the bottom line and Lily as someone lower down the hierarchy who just wants an easy life, we could re-write the scene like this:

Fred stands at the printer admiring the quality of his latest documents and blocking Lily's access.

> LILY
> Fred? Fred?

> FRED
> Ooh, sorry. I really think having this print quality in-house is going to save us a bomb on outsourcing.

> LILY
> Yeah, well I'm only interested in the time it saves me, so get a wriggle on.

You can see that just by making the dialogue motivated, that is to say tied to character and the desires of those characters, there's an immediate improvement.

Of course, exposition, while a necessary evil in drama, is a valid method of teaching. When writing a learning drama it's important that any exposition is there to support the dramatic structure, not as an end in itself. Drama is not a good vehicle for expositional learning.

Part 2: Description

When we write video description, we are trying to evoke the feeling of watching a film. It's not dissimilar to writing audio description for a visually impaired audience. You need to be concise, or it will spoil the flow of listening. And you must leave something for the director, actors and crew to do. They are, after all, interpreting your work.

Video description is called "action" because everything you describe is active - driving your plot forward. The objects in your scenes are narrative devices. A boiling kettle suggests bubbling emotion. A car moves characters around but also provides a means of expression when we see how they drive. Maybe a character feels trapped in their car? Or is it a status symbol?

Your nouns should be precise. Not a 'luxury sports car, a 'Porsche'. Not a "nail", a "tack". Not a "dog", a Labrador.

And because everything we describe is active let's make it feel like that. Not – "There is a Porsche in the drive", rather "A

Porsche stands on the drive." It's standing, it's active! It could equally be resting, that's still an action.

Never use metaphors in your description – the objects and actions in a scene are the metaphors.

Resist the temptation to write "we see" – this describes the act of viewing rather than evoking the experience. Instead, vividly describe what is happening, right now, as we live this filmic experience together.

Don't write camera directions unless you really have to. You are the writer, not the director. Write what you want the viewing experience to be and trust your director to bring that experience to the screen.

Learning designers often can't resist the temptation to "design" the film, leading to an overuse of conspicuous devices such as split screen, rewind and literal point-of-view. These might fly well when pitched to a client, but are rarely as effective as the inconspicuous filmic techniques used by trained directors. Trust your director.

Using the fewest words possible, description lays out the visual elements of film. We don't describe every tiny movement of an actor, rather the ones that offset the dialogue to tell the story.

                              AUDREY
          Come on Danny, when are you
          going to sort yourself out?
          It's been six months now.

     Danny says nothing, just taps at his
     keyboard.

These eight words of description give us three points of
information and a wealth of emotional insight.

Keep dialogue interchange alive with tiny observations.

     Fred sighs - it's all been for nothing.

     Victoria smiles - it's better than she
     expected.

     Sabine holds eye contact.

     Simon rubs his chin.

Do not expect the cast and director to interpret your directions
literally. A chin rub is probably too hammy a gesture to indicate
thinking, but the actor will find another way to express it.

Of course, a video written for learning is not a movie. Large
organisations have special needs. We sometimes have to
add what one might describe as 'contractually necessary
description'. Compliance must be respected.

Learning Points

Dialogue is written after the story is designed.

- Where you can get away with not writing any dialogue, do so!

- Dialogue is messy.

- People don't say what they mean.

- People don't say what they would like to say.

- Dialogue doesn't sound nice.

- Write short speeches.

- Read your dialogue aloud.

- Use suspense structure.

- Use different voices for each character.

- Don't put learning points into the mouths of characters.

- Dramatize exposition.

Video description:

- Video description aims to evoke the feeling of watching a film.

- Use precise language.

- Everything you describe is active, an actor in the video.

- Never use metaphors, the objects and actions you describe are metaphors.

- Don't write "we see", this describes the act of viewing rather than evoking the experience.

- Avoid writing camera directions.

- Keep dialogue interchange alive with small observations.

7.

Formatting

> **"Always do things in the least interesting way, and you make a better movie."**
>
> – David Mamet

A script is set of instructions for how to make a film, so naturally there are some technical specifications to work to. Screenwriting format is a powerful tool that is easily overlooked. It has been evolving for over a century and took a massive leap forward when in 1914 Tomas Ince used it to revolutionize filmmaking.

Thought of as the Henry Ford of movie production, Ince commissioned a new scriptwriting format that would have a range of practical functions – from selling the project to costing. A document that would serve at all stages of the production process called the continuity script. This new tool allowed him to run many projects simultaneously and productivity soared.

94   CONTINUED: (1)   ILSA
                       (softly)
         Sam, play it once for old time's
         sake.

                          SAM
         I don't know what you mean, Miss
         Ilsa.

                          ILSA
         Play it, Sam. Play "As Time Goes By."

                          SAM
         I can't remember it, Miss Ilsa!

Of course he can. He doesn't want to play it. He seems
even more scared.

                          ILSA
         I'll hum it for you.
                       (starts to hum)

He begins to play it very softly.

                          ILSA
         Sing it, Sam.

And Sam sings.

                          SAM
         "You must remember this,
         A kiss is still a kiss,
         A sigh is just a sigh..."
         Etc., etc.

95   ENTRANCE TO GAMBLING ROOM - RICK

       - comes swinging out. He has heard the music and he is
       livid.
                          RICK
         Sam, I thought I told you never to play it!

He stops abruptly, stops speaking and stops moving.

96   FROM HIS PERSPECTIVE - SAM & ILSA
       - at the piano.

97   CLOSER ANGLE - SAM & ILSA
       Sam looks over his shoulder at Rick and stops playing.
       Ilsa knows why even before she turns and looks. She knows
       who she'll see when she turns. She turns slowly. She
       isn't breathing much.

98   CLOSEUP - RICK
       - isn't breathing at all. It's a wallop, a shock. For a
       long moment he just looks at her and you can tell what he
       is thinking. He starts moving forward, his eyes riveted
       on her. CAMERA TRUCKS AHEAD of him, keeping him in
       CLOSEUP as he moves across the cafe.

A page from the script of Casablanca, written in continuity script format.

The modern Hollywood format is the master script, which has developed just a little, to put more emphasis on readability. This is what the writer produces, and it is later further developed by the director and producer, with more practical annotation, into a shooting script – making it more like a continuity script.

In L&D we use a slight adaptation of the master script. Here is an example with format elements labelled:

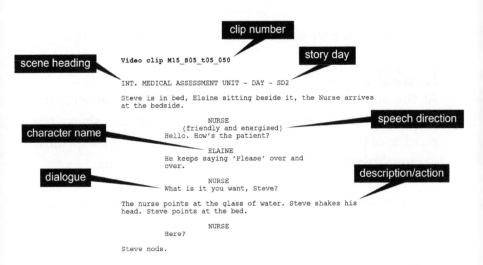

The format elements are as follows:

Clip number

Not a movie script format element – but essential in most learning content. Clip numbers are needed to integrate the video content within the structure of the learning experience whether that's face-to-face or online. If you don't have clip numbers, call the clips something – clip 1, clip 2 etc. We need to know what we're talking about.

Scene heading

This comprises:

- INT OR EXT (interior or exterior)
- Location
- Time of day (usually as simple as "DAY")

We know where we are and roughly what time of day it is.

Story Day

At the end of the scene heading is a little number with the prefix "SD" standing for "story day". This number shows the passing of time across a series of scenes – and manifests most obviously with characters wearing different clothes.

Leave it off if the passage of time is not relevant to your content.

Description/Action

Every video scene should begin with description before dialogue. Who is in the room? How are they positioned? This helps the production team if they record the scenes in non-narrative order.

Very occasionally one needs to put in a camera direction. The word CAMERA should be in capitals to draw attention to this. Shot sizes, such as CLOSE-UP should also be in caps.

Character name

These should be in capitals, making them quickly recognizable. Character names must be consistent throughout the script.

Speech directions

In brackets below the character name. These refer to the way something is said (sarcastic) rather than any action the speaker is making simultaneously (shaking head) which should be formatted as an action.

Dialogue

Insofar as a script is a set of instructions to create a video, dialogue is no exception. For example, it's useful to write numbers in full to ensure the speech matches the intention of the writer. "One thousand and one" rather an "1001", which could also be voiced as "one double zero one".

If you are writing a scene in which one character interrupts the speech of another, a useful device is to put a few words that they would have said if they weren't interrupted in brackets at the end of their speech, and to add the speech direction "cutting in" before the next speech.

```
                    BRIAN
         I've got a really interesting
         script I'd like to tell you
```

```
           about (all about aliens from
           the planet Bing).

                    VERA
                 (cutting in)
           Just bring me the coffee would
           you waiter.
```

This gives actors a through-line which can improve performance and save time on set.

If a character is heard but not seen, write "O.S." for "off screen", after the character name on the same line.

The master script format is used for movie production and you can buy and get free software designed to work with it. TV script formats differ, but they have more or less the same elements for the same pragmatic reasons.

Learning Points

- A script is a set of instructions to make a film, so you must stick to the technical specifications.

- The master script is the standard script format used in Hollywood.

- Follow the format guidelines from this chapter when you write a drama script.

- Software for writing in master script format is available to buy and for free, but you can use any word processing software.

8.

Script review

"The first draft of anything is shit".

— Ernest Hemmingway.

Scripts for an eLearn are routinely offered to stakeholders to make corrections directly into the text to ensure the content is compliant. This works fine for eLearning but it's inappropriate for video drama scripts even if they are destined for an eLearn. When it occurs, it can lead to absurd dialogue that's 100% compliant with corporate policy, but not credible as drama.

The solution is to allow only comments on a drama script, and for these to be honoured and interpreted by the writer.

Learning Point

- eLearning scripts are usually distributed to the stakeholders for them to make amends directly to the document. This doesn't work for drama scripts, so invite comments instead.

9.

The real world of L&D

– George Lucas

O ccasionally in L&D we are fortunate enough to make a drama with a complete story arc and well-developed characters in a lovely long video. But this is rare. The most common forms of dramatic video in learning are:

- Short standalone clips
- Short clips from a longer story
- Short clips from a longer story arranged in an interactive, branching course.

Short standalone clips

To get the most from a standalone clip, imagine a complete story from which it is a slice. Let's say you are briefed to write

By Mike_shots - Shutterstock

a short clip about a woman thief, designed to help police empathize with their suspects. I'd ask myself, "What did she do to become a suspect? What will become of her? Is she really a criminal, or is she innocent?" At once a complete story is springing to mind. Take this story and shape it further with the dramatic tools.

Who was this woman's opponent? What was the inciting incident that began the chain of events? What was she like before she found herself caught in the act? Once she takes a misstep what are the progressive complications that lead to her becoming a thief? After the theft what happens to her? The climax and the resolution.

I imagined a middle-class single mother falling victim to online fraud. She tries to get by - taking all the part time work she can, but still can't feed her children. She feels compelled to shoplift. She is arrested and given probation. This serves as a cry for help and the police support her in recovering her lost funds.

With this sketch of a complete story, you can choose which bit of it to portray to best serve your objective. If you plumped for the arrest scene it might look dramatic but is likely to be somewhat superficial. You'd get more depth from a scene if you chose to represent the moment when she decides to go shoplifting, or the police interview after the arrest.

Imagine your audience peering into your imagined world through a tiny window. They can see deep, but not wide. With small details you can suggest a world beyond the edge of frame. This is one reason to write more than you can use. A full picture is in your mind and it oozes into a scene.

© Sueddeutsche Zeitung Photo / Alamy Stock Photo

Make your scenery deep to suggest a world beyond the edge of frame.

Often, standalone learning clips are realized as lightweight comedy sketches. In this short format, comedy is often easier to pull off than straight drama. Comedy is naturally heightened and lends itself to conceptual narratives. However, it is not as emotionally engaging as drama. In the next chapter I deal with how the foregrounding technique present in comedy can work to benefit learning.

Short clips from a longer story
Sometimes courses are designed around a group of clips that are scenes from a longer story. They do, in fact, tell a complete story, but because the duration is short, the effect is of a series of moments from a longer film.

Whenever there are several drama clips needed in a course, I advise that we try to link them as a complete story. A complete story is bound to be a synergistic choice. You need less time to establish the characters and their relationships, allowing more time for drama. Viewers can get to know a character, better to see things from their point of view. The whole thing is more of an emotional journey, which also makes it more memorable. There are challenges of course. Can the issues you wish to touch upon in your course be mapped nicely across the arc of a story to fit within the modular learning structure? Or can you be a bit loose about how the drama relates to the rest of the learning?

As well as in a standard eLearning course, short clips from a longer story work well in a MOOC, (massive open online course), where drama is a powerful means to stimulate discussion. You don't need to resolve a story; it can be more productive to depict unresolved dilemmas and challenges.

Short clips from a longer story arranged in an interactive, branching course.

This format is dealt with fully in chapter 11. For now, it will suffice to say it is a story spanning across a series of clips, but every time the user makes a choice the story veers in one direction or another. So, you have many versions of the same story.

Due to budget constraints, we are often asked to produce to-camera monologues, (a single character talking directly to the camera). Often there are a number of these spread across a course. The main thing to know about designing monologues is that, although they feature a single character, they are nevertheless subject to the same rules as any other drama. The story techniques are the same, as is subtext and all the other drama elements described here.

So, ask yourself how you can get conflict and story into your monologues. One way is to for the character to recount a complete story. Another is to have them in conflict with themselves - so there is a tension between what they say and what we, the audience, perceive to be the truth. We can also have them working out their relationship to recounted events as they relate them. What a dramatic monologue is not, is exposition.

Drama vs role-play

In L&D we are often called upon to depict a scenario for demonstration purposes. Do we make it a role-play or a drama? It's important to choose the form in which you are working.

Suppose you are writing for volunteers at a mental health help line. The piece shows a volunteer taking a call from a distressed person and illustrates 100% correct practice. You think of it as a demonstration, so you write a role-play. But because of the subject matter, the content is, nevertheless, emotional, so it could be perceived as a drama, with all the expectations that brings. This could lead to a disappointed, and therefore disengaged audience. To help it read as a role-play – step back from realism and film it as a clear demonstration. This is a rational look at an emotional situation.

In practice, of course, the emotions of volunteers are affected by such interactions. So, we may want to speak to their emotional selves. And to do that we write a drama. Now the emotions of our protagonist, the volunteer, become the central subject matter. The structure is built to engage these constructively. Most likely, we aim the piece at a dilemma. Then bring to bear the rest of the techniques in this book.

Be aware that the distinction between role-play and drama is often disregarded when the subject matter is less emotive, but the principles still apply.

Learning Points

There are 3 main forms of drama video in learning:

- Short standalone clips
- Short clips from a longer story
- Short clips from a longer story arranged in an interactive, branching course.

- Standalone clips are sometimes a fragment from a longer story. They can also be lightweight comedy sketches.

- Small details can suggest a story world beyond the edge of frame.

- Making a collection of clips part of a longer story presents opportunities for character development and greater audience engagement.

- Short clips arranged in an interactive, branching scenario usually portray different versions of the same story to enable exploration of an issue. (See chapter 11).

- Be clear as to whether your video is a role-play or a drama.

WATCH & LEARN

10.

Foregrounding and Commentary

"Comedy is not supposed to be funny. It's supposed to tell the truth and then that's funny."

– Paula Patton

Learning demands two types of attention from an audience. The first is emotional attention. This is where drama excels. The second is analytical attention. What is this drama showing me and how do I critically relate to it? Tools to engage people in this discussion include text in an eLearn, a face-to-face experience or a talking head video. But sometimes criticism of the drama comes from within it – which is what this chapter is about. Every time we bring a learner into an analytical mindset, we push them away from emotional engagement. So, it's important to carefully balance these two forms of attention in any drama-based learning.

Sometimes we incorporate a commentary within a drama – criticizing the content as we go. Criticism pushes us out of the dramatic space, and we view the action at a distance.

This is the 'alienation effect', also known as the distancing or estrangement effect. Bertolt Brecht first used the term in an essay on "Alienation Effects in Chinese Acting" published in 1936, in which he described actors "playing in such a way that the audience was hindered from simply identifying itself with the characters in the play. Acceptance or rejection of their actions and utterances was meant to take place on a conscious plane, instead of, as hitherto, in the audience's subconscious". I call these effects 'foregrounding' because they bring forward the artifice. Brecht harnessed the technique to heighten his audience's critical faculties ready to receive a revolutionary message. Seems like it might also work for us.

Comedy is based on criticism with laughter as an expression of a critical position. We stand back to laugh at things. This is why - be our content funny or serious – we can borrow from comedy's many foregrounding techniques. A character turns and speaks directly into camera - breaking the fourth wall.

© Nice Media

A chance to deliver a judgement on the action, unheard by its characters. Often, it's a mentor who addresses us. They disrupt our suspension of disbelief like a reflective and rational inner voice. So, it makes perfect sense to put your moral message into their mouth.

Another foregrounding technique is the character with an inner voice — "Who am I to be writing a book? My dad was a plumber, and I went to comprehensive school." This is very similar to addressing camera, but the thoughts are expressed subjectively, not socially filtered. So, you'd be less likely to use this for an official line on the content, rather to encourage critical thinking.

We can do a similar thing with captions - spelling out what's *really* going on in a scene.

There's a further technique, often employed in learning that incorporates commentary into drama - the flashback.

© Nice Media

"I was such a fool to let myself get scammed. It was an ordinary working day when someone phoned me from a number I didn't recognize."

The form consists of a character talking to camera, or to another character, and then we see her acting out some of the scenes she describes. The principle reason for flashbacks in movies is to deliver exposition – so we should remember that they aren't all that dramatic. So, if you do choose this form, try to liven it by making the narrative surprising. We already know the end of the story, so how we arrived there is the only part remaining where we can delight and surprise.

Funnily enough, a great way to combine all the great comedic techniques I've described is to make a comedy. And why not? People are often cautious about using comedy because they fear their audience is too easily offended or won't laugh at the same things. How can we ensure it is suitable for an international audience?

Another way to look at it is that comedy is a great means to discuss delicate issues and theoretical concerns with a light touch. Think of the classic sitcom Seinfeld. It's a modern comedy of manners and morality. In every episode the characters try to figure out how to behave in modern society. The story structure is:

1. Identify and label the problem.
2. Try to outsmart the problem.
3. The problem outsmarts you.

Issues dealt with include – whether to give your fiancée your ATM card code; how to split up with an old friend; saying "Nice to meet you" to someone you've previously met.

Comedy drama takes an idea and tests it to extremes. We don't read it as realism; we know it's comedy, so we know the discussion of serious issues is heightened. The knots that sitcom characters tie themselves into when they try to get around doing the right thing are not realistic, but they feel right because we all do silly things in awkward situations.

"No hugging. No learning." – Larry David

Learning Points

- Drama for learning must balance the command of two types of audience attention – emotional and analytical.

- Commentary can be incorporated into drama, making us stand back and think about what we're watching.

- Bertolt Brecht famously coined the term "alienation effect" in 1936, I prefer the term "foregrounding".

- Comedy is based on criticism, so its techniques can be adopted to create foregrounding in drama.

- Foregrounding techniques include:
    - A character addressing the camera
    - A character's inner voice
    - Text on screen
    - Flashbacks

- Much comedy is about critical discussion of ideas, so if you can master the form, it's great for learning.

11.
Interactive branching scenarios

"Trying to solve a problem before being taught the solution leads to better learning, even when errors are made in the attempt. "

Make it Stick – Brown, Roediger & McDaniel.

Effortful learning in the form of problem solving is far more effective than being spoon-fed a solution. This is how interactive, branching scenarios engage your conscious brain. The emotional aspect of video scenarios, though, can work even when the learner is apparently passive (in fact emotionally active). As described in the preceding chapters – video drama allows us to see the world as others see it, and the lessons learnt in that way can be effective, deep, and instantaneous.

So, the art of the interactive, branching scenario is to keep these two types of attention in balance. We need to involve people in the characters, their situations, and emotions, while simultaneously keeping them actively thinking, and intellectually engaged. Get it right and it is incredibly effective. Get it wrong and you can fail on both counts. Let's look at some of the conflicting demands.

Story arc: Creating a single, satisfying story about a few characters and a given issue is challenge enough. In an ideal branching scenario, we would have a plethora of perfectly satisfying stories, all of which begin in the same way, but develop and end very differently. In practice, without an enormous budget, this means we often end up with a 'shallow' branching structure. With sleight of hand, we can give the impression of more branches than there really are.

Exploration: We want learners to explore as much of our content as possible – it's better value for money. So, we can't let scoring drive the interactivity lest it inhibit this exploration. If learners only see the optimal narrative path, they can sail through without learning about what can go wrong. Here the balance is between making the learning effortful so the decision points are memorable, while encouraging playful exploration.

Developing this theme – the multiple-choice questions can't be too tough or complicated lest they inhibit the learner's flow. When we interrupt viewing with a question, the question should be pertinent to what they've just seen, succinctly written with simple choices. A yes/no response is great for flow.

Multiple-choice alone is a weak learning tool – it's not very sticky. But here the multiple-choice questions function as a steering mechanism to focus the learner's thinking while they watch a scene. They are not the core of the learning, the video is.

To help keep our learner's attention nicely balanced between emotion and analysis, it helps if the video clips are short. This is not at all easy, and the story is best heightened in one way or another. Foregrounding, making the drama a self-conscious one, perhaps with an inbuilt commentary, keeps the learner closer to an analytical position. This fits nicely with the mental adjustment needed to play the interactive game, but also means their engagement with the characters will be less emotional.

Foregrounding can also be achieved if we heighten our drama to a melodrama by increasing the emotional pitch, which also makes it less realistic. Or we can heighten with comedy – which allows for compression because it is so conceptual. Comedy puts audiences in a critical relationship to the content, keeping their head closer to an analytic mode.

One foregrounding technique we often see is literal point of view – putting the camera in the position of the protagonist. This is mistakenly thought to be dramatically immersive. In fact, the technique draws attention to itself and puts the viewer in a critical position.

Some subject matter is better suited for a literal point-of-view approach. A well-known interactive piece about knife crime "Choose a Different Ending" is filmed from a literal point of view and yet feels quite emotionally immersive.

In a violent altercation we are pumped with adrenaline. We are suddenly completely analytically *and* emotionally engaged with the problem of how we should respond to the threat. At the same time, our visual awareness is heighted and literal point of view is a good analogue for this.

A well-known interactive course combines literal point of view with light comedy - this is Will You Fit into Deloitte — a recruitment film about company values. The subject of corporate values is a serious one, and, as it very much involves the overlap of the private and public, is also sensitive. Here it benefits from a light touch. The foregrounding afforded by literal point of view sits well with the light comedy script and it all works nicely with the interactivity.

Another way to make courses an agile experience is to keep the agenda of learning points short. It's not easy to keep an audience's attention intellectually and emotionally at the same time. If we overladen the design and the script with a plethora of content, the result will be stodgy at best.

Drama, remember, is more about depth than breadth. As we develop the story, it naturally becomes more complex than we first imagined, and more learning points are introduced.

An interactive branching course aspires to have both learning interactions and drama that are quick and effective, to keep the user in the perfect head space.

One design ploy we can use to support this is to precede the interactive part of the video with a linear piece. This introduces the characters and the situation and gets the audience aware of the issues at stake before we switch gear and ask them to become involved with the narrative.

Learning Points

- The art of interactive, branching drama is to keep analytical and emotional attention balanced.

- Writing a single story is hard enough, but creating several variations on the same story is tough.

- Encouraging the exploration of as much of the content as possible is at odds with the demands of points-driven gamification.

- Multiple choice questions should be short and not too difficult to encourage flow.

- Individual clips should be short to encourage flow.

- The foregrounding techniques discussed in chapter 10 are often appropriate here.

- Literal point-of-view is a foregrounding technique.

- Keep the list of learning points short.

- Precede the interactive drama with a linear one to help establish character, setting and story.

12.

Costs

D rama is one of the most expensive forms of video. To make the most of your budget it's essential to design a solution that takes account of cost factors. So, let me explain the key cost considerations for designing drama-based video learning.

© Julie Edwards

One day at a time

A 10-hour day, with an hour for lunch, is the baseline unit around which we design a production. A drama crew charges in units of days. Actors also charge a day rate, and the equipment we'll need is hired out in the same units. So, it makes sense to design a production that gets the optimum from the number of days we can afford.

Usually, we get around 10 minutes of drama from a day's filming, but in special circumstances we have produced up to 25 minutes. At the other end of the production spectrum, Hollywood movies shoot closer to a minute a day – that's how much attention to detail a movie gets.

Size of cast

Scenes with a smaller cast are quicker to film than scenes with more speaking parts. In terms of duration of output, the smaller the cast, the more productive you will be. There are less people to manage, and the visual storytelling is simplified. Also there will be fewer fees to pay.

© Nice Media

Actor days

We might, though, have several scenes, each involving two actors, but a different pair in each scene. This is still relatively quick to film, but it will cost more, because actors charge by units of a day. Even with a fifth of the lines, an actor will still expect a full fee.

Think in units of actor-days. Actor fees are a significant element of the budget and are compounded with travel, costume and other expenses related to each cast member, plus the pre-production time necessary to cast them.

Casting

It takes time and skill to find a cast to fit the bill. They need to be good and willing to work for corporate rates. One weak player can let down the whole show – so getting the casting right is key. Casting is a worthwhile investment.

Story days

The events in a story often happen over a number of days. To express the change between one story-day and another, there is usually a change of:

- costume
- makeup
- lighting
- props

Each of these takes time. So, if you can tell your story with less story days you will achieve efficiencies.

Set-ups

Moving all the kit and crew around while filming takes time. Even something as simple as moving from filming at one desk to another in the same room takes a significant chunk out of the day. Each new arrangement of camera and lights around a focal point is called a 'set-up'. The more set-ups you have, the more visually rich your film can be. However, more set-ups is less productive than fewer.

When moving from one building to another, or moving inside to outside, we are paying our assembled team of experts to be porters, not artisans. Shoots with the highest output feature a small cast in a single location.

Number of cameras

The number of cameras used is a choice to be made by the director and producer, but it is worth knowing that nowadays, drama is often filmed with 2 or more cameras simultaneously. This brings its own challenges and restrictions – needing more crew and more money for equipment, but the productivity boost is often worth it.

Production values

The glossier the production the more it costs. Gloss, or production value can be attained through a variety of means all of which boil down to attention to detail. This is achieved with more time to script, plan and film a drama – with the scripting and planning reaping the biggest cost return for a fixed investment.

© Nice Media

More time for lighting design, more camera angles, more tracking shots, great makeup and hair, beautiful costumes, stunning locations, budget for set or travel - all this investment increases the production value and makes your film look more Hollywood, but it all costs more money.

Studio vs location

© Nice Media

Often, with corporate filming, the client can provide premises in which to film. A meeting room, a corner of an open-plan office, an oil derrick, or a bus. This is effectively a free asset for the production. Locations though, are potentially noisy and ungovernable. Your well-paid team of cast and crew can be held up while Sam from accounts does an important run of noisy printing in the room where you're trying to film. That's a dent in the productivity that we must plan for.

A studio, on the other hand, is sound-proofed and has no external light sources. It is a completely controlled environment. Productivity can be very high. However, studios cost money – and that's before we've even talked about building a set. It's a fine judgement, but sometimes the studio will be the most cost-effective option.

Post-production

We've just seen the cost factors of production, what about post-production? A chief factor is the number of editing days needed. Poor, undisciplined directing can make an editor's job harder and take longer. The use of special effects, graphics, or dense cuts between many sources also eats up editing resources. Licencing stock footage and music, of course, also has a cost.

You can't beat a well-designed, planned and filmed drama, which will be straightforward to edit, with the footage fitting together like a jigsaw.

The reality

Of course, we don't want to make loads of dramas involving just one or two characters in a single setting. What fun we'd miss! The same goes for story days and tracking shots and all the nice things that are a pleasure to watch. The art is to come up with designs that allow you get the most from each day of filming, that will work with a few locations and a modest cast to tell a big story.

Learning Points

It's important to know the key cost considerations for designing drama. Cost factors include:

- A filming day - the basic unit of cost

- Size of the cast

- Actor days – number of actor's fees payable

- Casting

- Story days

- Set-ups

- Production values

- Studio vs location

- Number of days to edit

- Licencing of any stock items – music or footage.

13.

Filming: what happens on set

"Filmmaking is the ultimate team sport."
– Michael Keaton

The hierarchy

On a film set there is a hierarchy, and we all work together, very intensely, in beautiful harmony with this understanding keeping us efficient. Let's have a look at how it works.

Producer

The producer and her team oversee the management of the project. They have contracted everyone on the shoot and now they have brought them all together to work to a schedule.

Director

The producer is the boss of the director in terms of time and budget, but the director is boss in terms of how the scenes are filmed.

The director has likely chosen the cast and oversees the performances and how they are delivered. The producer's team will have brought talent on set, in the correct outfit at the correct time, but it's up to the director to tell them where to stand, which lines to speak and how they are framed by the camera.

© Nice Media

Talent

Acting involves bringing your own real emotion to the work. So, part of the job of the director is to shelter the actors from the pressures that surround them. If they fluff their lines, they are holding up an expensive wagon train. The director needs to make concerns go away and allow the actors to become immersed in the imaginary world of the script. In short, actors need to play and everyone else needs to work.

The crew play along with the director to support this atmosphere. It is one reason why there can seem to be an excess of levity on a film set. The banter can be fun, but it can obscure our intense process to the casual eye.

Camera & lighting

The director is also in charge of what's in the camera frame. She will work closely with a director of photography. This is the technician in charge of the placement and operation of the lighting and cameras. In a Hollywood shoot, a DoP, as we say, won't operate a camera personally, but on our productions they would.

Lighting is technical, but it's also artful. "Painting with light" is how it's often described. Lighting can give a mood, show the passing of time, can lead our eye, can be realistic or fantastic.

© Julie Edwards

Sound

A sound recordist may be alone or have assistants - someone to share the boom swinging and audio mixing tasks while the drama is performed. As well as the task of getting clean dialogue recordings, the sound team support the director – ensuring we have all the sound assets needed at the edit stage. This might include recording segments of apparent silence to help sound continuity.

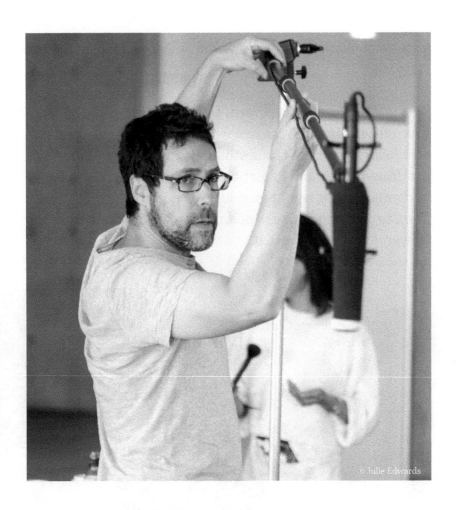

© Julie Edwards

Hair and makeup

Why do we even have hair and makeup technicians for actors, when they come into to room looking perfectly acceptable? At the most basic level if we didn't pay attention to an actor's appearance it would soon draw remarks and become a distraction. More importantly, hair and makeup bring out aspects of character that draw the audience deeper into the story world.

We must not forget that, even if this story is meant to be set in your office, this is not the real world; it's a heightened version of it. Every aspect of the aesthetic is given extra shine so as not draw attention to the artifice. The audience unconsciously understands the heightened look of a film and that directs them to go along with us and invest in the fiction with all the conventions that go with it.

© Julie Edwards

Costume

Costume works in the same way. It needs to look attractive and unremarkable, unless the remarkable element deepens our understanding of character or story.

Location, set and props

Finding somewhere to film is a major resource for our budgets. That is why so many corporate films are shot on location at the client's premises. At other times, we film at a hired location or at a film studio.

A location may need some props to make it suitable to tell our story. Perhaps signage needs to be translated to mimic a foreign land?

When filming in a studio, sometimes we don't even use a set – instead filming against white to give the video a more heightened and abstracted look and feel. We still need some props though – chairs and tables and laptops and angle poises. Remaining in this abstract zone, more and more background props can be added to give the scene depth.

The next step is to build a complete set, to decorate it and to dress it with props. The complete creation of a fictional setting.

As with all the other departments, our endeavours serve the storytelling. Like the other departments, they take their creative orders from the director and the managerial ones from the producer.

© Nice Media

WATCH & LEARN

Attending a shoot

As a client or consulting learning designer on a set for the first time it can feel a bit disorienting – it's a new world! Your producer will give you a front row seat, so you can see the scenes going down. You will be advised by the director, ensuring you understand how each shot will fit into the construction of the whole film. You will be asked for your opinion on the performances. Make sure to only give your feedback through the director and not directly to the cast. Part of a director's job is to take what may be contradictory suggestions from members of the client team and convert them into simple, playable actions. It's all part of helping the actors stay playful – which makes for a better performance.

The director uses three main techniques to adjust a performance:

1. Active verbs:
Actors don't be, they do. Actors are active. You'd never tell an actor to "be more angry," you'd say "attack her" or "insult him". Tease, defend, flirt, complain. Active verbs are more specific than nouns and describe the action that you want to see.

2. Adjustments:
- "Play it like mother and son"
- "It's like you're playing poker and know you have a winning hand"

- "Just before this scene you've had a row with your partner"
- "You're in a hurry."

3. Exploration of contextual meaning:

What does 'accruals' mean? Why is Helen tired all the time? If this meeting goes well for you there's every chance your character will be promoted.

Learning Points

- Film sets run on a clear hierarchy that serves productivity.

- The producer oversees management of the project.

- The director is in charge of how the scenes are filmed.

- Other functions include:
  - Acting
  - Director of Photography (DoP)
  - Sound
  - Hair and Makeup
  - Costume
  - Location, Set and Props

- If you think of the hierarchy like a great big machine, as a consulting learning designer or visiting client, your access to it is via the producer and director.

- Directors work with actors using:
  - Active verbs
  - Adjustments
  - Exploration of contextual meaning

14.

Editing

> **"To receive footage that has been shot with editing in mind, it is a blessing."**
>
> *– Thelma Schoonmaker*

As I described in the section on dialectics – editing creates meaning by juxtaposing images and sounds to create concepts in the viewer's imagination. But the material of the editor has already been created by the writer, the director and production team. So, is the editor just assembling a kit of short clips of video according to a predetermined plan?

Even if there only exist close shots on one part of a scene and wide shots for the remainder, the editor can still bring their skills to bear. The editor cuts between faces. They don't follow the lines, flip-flopping like a tennis match, they follow the emotion. Remember, the conversation is rarely about what is being said, it is about the emotional exchange. So, an editor will often show one character listening while the other speaks because at that moment, that reaction is the most important thing emotionally.

The emotional exchange of a scene is first designed in the script. This is developed in the mind of the director. When it comes to filming it may take a new turn in light of the performances. Now, in the edit suite, the editor can uncover these performances and even change them – altering the rhythm and chopping between takes.

Despite this new layer of innovation, if the director has done their job well, and communicated clearly to the client, the client gets the film that they imagined. Or at least, a film that does what they imagined. So, client feedback in response to the first cut is often minimal.

When the first edit is delivered, it rarely has a complete sound mix or a full grade. So, bear in mind the video is still to be enhanced in these respects.

The sound mix should make all the voices clear and even, and smooth out any clunks and hisses. Sound effects and music may also be added.

Grading is the final adjustment of the colour and tonality to make all the shots look their best, and cut together with visual consistency. Grading can bring a particular feel to a video scene – making it look more gritty, warm, modern or aged.

Learning Points

- Editing creates meaning by juxtaposing images and sound to create concepts in the viewer's imagination.

- When editing a conversation an editor will follow the emotion, not the words.

- The first draft of an edit often has not been graded, nor is the sound mix final. So, it may lack contrast and the sound might be rough.

- Grading can be used to give a particular look – be that cool, warm, gritty or aged.

15.
Science notes

"Write what should not be forgotten."

– Isabel Allende

The single strength of drama I have championed is its ability to stimulate critical thinking. This is something that is hard to evaluate scientifically. I'm a filmmaker, not a scientist. My interest in science is to sense check assumptions that underlie my practice. I don't pretend to be a master of this material, but I thought it worth sharing a few notes and references that I have found interesting.

Your retention of the content of an instructional video is subject to Ebbinghaus' forgetting curve. You forget 50% of it within an hour, and the learning continues to fall away unless you watch/ listen again, take notes, etc. Drama, however, can confound this effect because the learning is bound up with emotion.

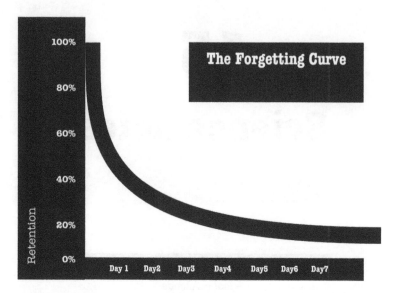

Diagram: Jonathan Swain

There is plenty of research to show that the more emotional an experience, the more vividly it is recalled. Some of this effect might be to do with the fact that when you've had an emotional experience, you tend to talk about it. Which fits in nicely with how we prefer to use corporate drama.

Our drama concerns emotional subjects and raises more questions than answers. It concerns the public/private overlap. This engages the audience emotionally and gets them thinking. We aim to leave them stimulated to discuss the issues - either within a facilitated experience, or at the water cooler

The challenge is to make a video that's as emotional as possible within the limits of the culture of the organisation.

In her book *Emotions, Learning and the Brain*, Mary Helen Immordino-Yang shows the magnitude of the neurological relationship between cognition and emotion using this Venn-like diagram.

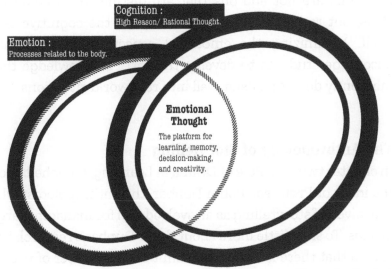

Diagram: Jonathan Swain

"It is literally neurobiologically impossible to build memories, engage complex thoughts, or make meaningful decisions without emotions"..."taken as a whole, [research studies] show that emotions are not just messy toddlers in a china shop, running around breaking and obscuring delicate cognitive glassware. Instead, [emotions] are more like the shelves underlying the glassware; without them cognition has less support" – Immordino-Yang

We only think deeply about the things we care about. Or, as Immordino-Yang puts it, "evidence suggests that meaningful learning is actually about helping students to connect their isolated algorithmic skills to abstract, intrinsically emotional, subjective and meaningful experiences"

Emotions are not add-ons that are distinct from cognitive skills, but rather become a dimension of the cognitive skill itself. Minimizing the emotional aspect of learning may encourage students to develop the sorts of knowledge that inherently do not transfer well into real-world situations.

The Anthropology of Storytelling
In chapter two, The Role of Drama in Learning, I touched upon the ideas of Professor Robin Dunbar, the anthropologist who conceived of storytelling as an evolved tool for managing large groups. To say a little more about this – Dunbar's research has shown that there is a cognitive limit to the number of people with whom one can maintain stable social relationships. This is known as 'Dunbar's number' and is around 150.

© Dan Dennis

A primate's chief method of social bonding is grooming, which functions by activating the brain's endorphin receptors. Dunbar theorized that since humans have much bigger social groups than other primates, we must be using more sophisticated bonding mechanisms than simple grooming. These include laughter, singing and dancing. These endorphin-stimulating activities give us a mental and physical "social high" that bond us.

Storytelling, with its emotional ups and downs, is another of these mechanisms that has developed, through novels and movies and such to a high level of sophistication. So, when we are delivering a story, fundamentally, we are engaging in a form of mass grooming!

In application, I suggest this works best if those consuming the story discuss it with their close colleagues and friends – leveraging intimate relationships to stimulate endorphins.

A workplace example would be the discussion of an emotional, dramatic scene in a MOOC or classroom setting.

The Power of Story

In his book *Flicker: Your Brain on Movies* (2004), Jeffrey M. Zacks writes:

"The social psychologist Carl Hovland studied the effects of Frank Capra's *The Battle of Britain* (1943), which was made to motivate US troops entering World War II in Europe (Hovland et al. 1949). Most important, Hovland found that although memory for facts decayed with time, some of the film's effects on attitudes grew over time - a pattern he dubbed the 'sleeper effect.'

Sleeper effects can occur when memory for information becomes dissociated from memory for the source of the information. Capra's recruits may have been sceptical of anything that came down from the army brass but after a while they just remembered his story, not its source."

Interactive, branching scenarios

Effortful learning is more sticky than low effort learning. This is the theme of *Make It Stick* by Peter C. Brown, Henry L. Roediger III, Mark A. McDaniel - a popular volume about the science of successful learning. This principle is clearly very applicable to interactive, branching scenarios.

"Trying to solve a problem before being taught the solution leads to better learning, even when errors are made in the attempt."

"It's trusting that trying to solve a puzzle serves us better than being spoon-fed the solution, even if we fall short in our first attempts at an answer."

"When learners commit errors and are given corrective feedback, the errors are not learned. Even strategies that are highly likely to result in errors, like asking someone to try to solve a problem before being shown how to do it, produce stronger learning and retention of the correct information than more passive learning strategies, provided there is corrective feedback."

Elizabeth and Robert Bjork, who coined the phrase 'desirable difficulties', write that, difficulties in learning are desirable because "they trigger encoding and retrieval processes that support learning, comprehension, and remembering." "To be desirable, a difficulty must be something learners can overcome through increased effort."

In *Scenario-based e-Learning: Evidence-Based Guidelines for Online Workforce Learning*, Ruth Clark suggests that scenario learning is probably most effective for people with some pre-existing knowledge of the subject and well-structured problems. She also says scenario-based learning appears to help people transfer what they learned to a new task and points out that problem-based learning seems to be more motivating.

Further Reading

This book doesn't have a bibliography, because most of it comes from a muddle of the hundred-odd books and courses I've studied over the years, all mixed up with putting it into practice. However, there are a couple of books I always go back to and these are *Story* by Robert McKee, the classic Hollywood screenwriter's reference, and John Truby's *The Anatomy of Story*, which brings McKee's models up to date. I'd also recommend *Three Uses of the Knife: On the Nature and Purpose of Drama* by David Mamet.

Learning Points

- You forget 50% of anything you learn within an hour, but drama can be an exception to this rule because of its emotional impact.

- Evidence suggests learning is about helping students to connect isolated skills to intrinsically emotional, subjective and meaningful experiences.

- Emotions are not add-ons that are distinct from cognitive skills, but rather become a dimension of the cognitive skill itself.

- Storytelling is an evolved tool to manage large groups.

- A study has shown that a feature film used as training created a memory of its story, independent of its source.

- With regard to interactive, branching scenarios, there is plenty of evidence to show that effortful learning is more sticky.

- Scenario learning works best for people with a pre-existing knowledge of the subject and well-structured problems.

16.

Case studies

When it comes to the application of theory and technique, we rarely have a blank canvas. Real life learning projects are complicated and messy. But once we have found the parameters we are working to, we can deploy theory to design content that is optimum.

First establish the function of the video drama content. This task alone is often deceptively challenging. There are often hidden assumptions about drama in learning. It is important to go back to the basics from earlier in this book and to reiterate what drama can and cannot achieve. If we forget that the main function of drama is moral and emotional rather than instructional in a mundane sense, we will be disappointed. The task of your drama must be defined in these terms: A drama sets out to give emotional insight, to stimulate critical thinking and to affect attitudes. It can also communicate a few high points of semantic learning, but these must be limited and bound up with the emotional message.

Function determined, what budget is available to us? What other assets do we have at our disposal? Resources defined, the design work begins.

Here are some real-life examples of what happened next.

Adult Safeguarding for Safeguarding Adults National Network and Health Education England.

Our clients had an ambitious aim. They needed to create a learning resource to serve half a million NHS safeguarding leads dispersed across England. There was currently no major learning asset to serve this function and they had a short timeframe to do this. They further challenged themselves by choosing to achieve this by producing their first ever MOOC, (massive open online course).

This was exciting for me because I'd long considered drama an excellent complement to a MOOC. Good learning drama stimulates conversation and that is exactly what is needed in a MOOC which is driven by social learning.

Working with our client in the development stage we had defined our resources as a cast of 6 to be filmed in a single day on location.

The function of the drama was not fully defined, so I began our collaboration by giving a presentation about the strengths and weaknesses of the medium.

Among the first suggestions we got for video scenarios were several that were intended to show the shocking effects of lack of safeguarding, namely violence and cruelty. Apart from the fact that such things are not very cost-effective to stage, my feeling was that, while they might be initially engaging, or at least attention-grabbing, they would do little to further our understanding of safeguarding.

After a lot of juggling with costs, and reflecting on the video content suggestions, I went back to the group and asked if there were ever meetings to establish what went wrong when a multidisciplinary team had failed to protect someone, and it had led to a death. There were, indeed, and I suggested this as the subject for the video content.

Such meetings bring together the various safeguarding professionals – from doctors to social workers to paramedics. They compare notes and records to piece together a coherent case narrative to present to a more formal meeting – a Safeguarding Adults Review.

This design choice allowed us to depict a highly emotional situation without the need for re-enactments of violence or abuse. In a powerful horror movie like Alien we don't see more than a hint of the monster until right at the end of the film. The horror is thus better evoked in the imagination of the viewer. By showing a multidisciplinary team discussing a death, each professional watching can reflect on how they might have found themselves in this situation, and of the impact that the death would have on them. In addition, this treatment would be cost-effective, allowing a lot of high-quality output from our day of filming. The solution also had the advantage that it would show multidisciplinary cooperation in action.

© Nice Media

The idea of making a film of a meeting sounds pretty dull, but this was going to be powerful. To give some variation, and to bring in some elements of exposition, we added intro and outro scenes consisting of vox pop style interviews with each character.

In the intro scenes they introduced themselves and said what they wanted from the meeting. In the outro scenes we asked the characters what they had learned. The latter served as a reiteration of some of the important learning points.

The next stage was to map the content of the meeting across the modules of the MOOC so that the relevant subject areas were dealt with as the story of the meeting unfolded.

The subject of the meeting became Sofia, a young woman who had been trafficked from Romania as a sex slave. She was made a heroin addict and her six-year-old daughter was threatened with acid to keep her compliant. Other problems manifested from her dysfunctional situation. She was found dead, a victim of violence.

The content of the meeting was written up in detail by one of our brilliant subject matter experts (SMEs), and this was the key document that our scriptwriter used to develop the script.

We also helped the SMEs to develop character descriptions which we used to cast and style our actors.

As the MOOC developed, Sofia's narrative thread was used to hang a lot of the learning on, a rewarding affirmation that we had chosen a productive route for the drama.

The MOOC was launched in January 2020 with over 6,000 (83%) of those who registered measured as active learners. Fully participating learners were measured at 56%.

This piece won the 2021 Training Zone Learning Excellence Award for Healthcare.

Points of Difference – multi-faceted drama reflecting workplace concerns

© Nice Media

One of the most amazing projects I've worked on occurred relatively early in my directing career. An international energy company had a new and innovative woman in their L&D department. Her vision was to produce a suite of dramas reflecting a wide range of reported workplace issues concerning points of difference. We depicted teams from offices across the globe with storylines set in Mumbai, Cairo, Moscow and Singapore.

The grand nature of the project allowed us to be subtle about how we treated the issues. There were 16 characters, with 4 in each location, plus a few extras. In each setting we had 6 scenes. So, that's 24 scenes with a total duration of just under 30 minutes. All this resource gave us a lot of possibilities. It's important to remember that, if you have a set of characters and a story that spans across a course, you can cram more learning into the clips because the depiction of setting and character can be established early on and shared across the piece. Following a group of people through stories that spanned several scenes, set across several months, allowed us to scope to develop characters. Each character had their own flaws and challenges, which entwined with those of other characters. We were able to explore issues sensitively, sympathetically, and realistically.

Some of the many topics we touched upon included in/out groups, cultural misunderstandings, feeling unable to speak up, underlying sexual tensions, an oil engineer dismissive of green issues, and a European woman feeling excluded in an Arab culture.

Scenes were filmed in the native language of the setting and subtitled. This made the videos work better across the global audience, but also supported the conceit that we had filmed internationally. In fact, everything was filmed at the company headquarters near London.

This major project, which could have easily been a white elephant - had it not been well-conceived, written and directed - proved to be so popular that people demanded to watch it in their own time. It was, after all, a depiction of their own lives and problems in a sympathetic, high quality drama.

The original intention of the films was as the core of a leadership course, but they were also re-used in other contexts including "town hall" meetings. This multi-pronged project with video at its core, led to change in the corporate culture whereby every meeting in the organisation kicked off with a moment of reflection about diversity.

The overall aim of the films was to stimulate productive, critical conversation about the issues raised. A task which was served admirably.

Moments of Truth – diversity discussion prompts for an international finance company

Our client approached us with a preconceived notion to create a suite of short videos designed to stimulate discussion around diversity and inclusivity. In many ways this was one of our easiest design processes because the client knew what they wanted and was familiar with similar projects we had produced elsewhere. Plus, we were all on the same page with drama and its best use. These were not to be training films, but rather films to enable critical discussion of issues surrounding race, disability, ageism, faith, negative self-talk, education, sexism, homophobia, and physical disability.

None of us imagined we could solve these problems with some little films, but we all believed that short videos, showing everyday examples of these issues, are a powerful tool to enable small teams, led by a manager working with detailed notes, to discuss these matters. It is evidenced that a culture in which discussion of difficult matters is made easy is a culture in which such issues become less problematic.

Our budget allowed 2 days filming and a cast of 11. We sketched out 9 scenes in treatment form. This is a half-page document that describes the action and characters. When we mapped this across the two-day shoot it was decided that we'd pushed the production envelope a little too much. One scene was removed, ensuring optimum quality for all scenes.

With all our scenes roughly designed, we needed to map our cast of 11 across the 21 characters. Each scene would be standalone, so there would be no problem re-using a cast member to play a different character. Eleven casting profiles (e.g. white Dutch male aged 40-50) were created to represent elements of the client's international workforce. These notional characters were then mapped across the scenes. We then offered the client a choice of actors to fit each role.

We were producing this during a pandemic, but we didn't want to restrict its shelf-life by making the cast wear masks. On the other hand, the pandemic had made remote working more prevalent and it seemed likely this would become the norm. So, we wrote 3 of the 8 scenarios as remote meetings.

© Nice Media

In a scene about ageism, we added an extra layer to our narrative by having the young interviewees of an older job candidate discuss her secretly during the interview via the chat function. This made the scene more dramatic and clearly drew attention to the prejudices we were seeking to depict.

Philip Clark 10:01 AM
She's not how I pictured her.

↩ Reply

Keisha Lewis 10:01 AM
Ditto.

↩ Reply

Remaining scenes were filmed in a white studio with minimal props and set. This treatment can work well with learning material because it makes it clear that this is fiction, while the drama is still all there. This means the viewer is not distracted by concerns relating to realism. In comparison, when a scene is set in your own workplace small inconsistencies with everyday reality can become disproportionately distracting. There is also the benefit that the video will age better.

© Nice Media

Pandemic precautions on set included all crew wearing masks, studio doors being opened between takes, cast socially distanced and a remote client who followed the action on Zoom.

IT Security – for an international pharmaceutical company

We had been working to develop video content for a course about IT security for our client. The production was all set to film when the Covid-19 pandemic arrived. The script featured a series of flashback scenarios in which four characters reflected on IT security slip-ups that had caused some kind of disaster. When the story is recounted flashback scenes cut into the testimony.

As the pandemic unfolded, we became practiced at filming within the restrictions of lockdown, but at this point we and the client agreed that filming as scripted was not going to be practicable, in particular the flashback scenes.

We re-wrote the story to film it remotely. The story was adapted to make it about 4 characters in an IT security working group that convened via a Microsoft Teams teleconference. Before the meeting can properly proceed, one of the delegates feels she must confess to an IT blunder that might disqualify her from the group. Her honesty inspires the others to tell their tales of woe and it becomes apparent that they have been recommended for the group because their understanding of the importance of the issues had been enhanced by their personal experiences.

A frame from IT Security

So, it became more like a little play – told in chunks that were interspersed across the eLearning course.

Forced to record remotely, we chose to make an advantage of it. While Zoom recordings produce low image quality, this is not necessarily something that inhibits engagement.

Studies have shown that audio quality is more important to viewers, providing the images are good enough to tell your story. Presenting a very convincing tele-conference image also had the advantage that the audience are used to being in these meetings themselves. So, the experience of viewing a clip is almost identical to that of being in such a meeting. Suspension of disbelief can thus click into place quite quickly.

The production was achieved practically by the following means:

- We secured a cast happy to use the tech.
- We spent time working technically with each actor to ensure they would be fine on the day of recording.
- We supervised costume choices remotely.
- We chose camera positions.
- We arranged background elements and lighting.
- We sent the cast audio recording devices with detailed instructions.
- We supervised sound deadening at each location.
- We supervised local screen recordings as backup.

A frame from IT Security – showing use of stock photo used to tell the story of a burglary being shared by one of the characters.

On the filming day we rehearsed for a time, called the client in to review the performances, then finally recorded the performances. Editing consisted largely of syncing our raw assets and assembling into chunks.

South Central Ambulance Service (SCAS) – Dementia Awareness Training

20 minutes of video to raise awareness of issues around dementia, aimed at ambulance staff.

SCAS already had a good deal of training material about dementia awareness, but none specifically designed for the ambulance service. Their idea was to show a patient pathway affecting a range of ambulance staff, from an emergency call taker to paramedics, drivers and patient transport service crew.

Although this is a procedural piece, we chose to stage it as a drama. Unlike a standard drama it's not written to bring out dilemmas. The real work of dealing with dementia has enough conflict, challenge and emotion to make it an appropriate drama rather than a role-play. Technically speaking, the video has a group protagonist (ambulance staff) with the antagonist being dementia rather than the individual with the condition. Dementia has a character – it is soulless and cruel and powerful, and it cannot be defeated. So, we must all learn to accommodate it.

© Nice Media

Take the opening scene: an emergency call taker is put through to an old man who has had a fall. We see the call from her point of view and only hear the man's voice. The call taker asks straightforward questions but gets strange, nonsensical answers. She tries her best to help the man, and all the time we hear the pain and confusion in his voice, while she remains calm and in control. At the end of the call, she has a few lines to let out her own feelings.

The ambulance staff featured don't need to emote very much, because it is their job to be cool in the face of emotional situations. But the patient and his family can be as emotional as we like because they represent the manifestation of the disease. We chose to keep the story very simple: a man has a fall, calls 999, is taken to hospital and returned home with his daughter on the scene. With a patient journey so naturally laden with drama, our job was to portray it with sensitivity, delivering learning points along the way.

Canon UK - IT security awareness

This project is not exactly drama as we've been discussing it, but comedy with a single actor.

We'd been approached by Brightwave who were working with Canon UK – providers of digital cameras, printers and so forth. They were developing a video-based campaign about IT security awareness. 12 short videos were needed as they were planning to release one a month for a year.

I'd recently been making some short comedy pieces – novelties really, designed to be distributed on mobile phones. Yes, it was quite a long time ago. The videos featured a performance by a single character filmed against black, with black velvet around the chin – giving the effect of a floating head. This allowed us to fly the head around in a lo-fi, but very effective way.

The idea seemed to be very suitable for this application, and we developed it so that a single performer played many characters who interacted with one another.

This heightened, comedic approach allowed us to present some of the more abstract ideas of IT security with a human face.

© Nice Media

The videos formed a yearlong 'viral' campaign to Canon staff around the world, deployed in multiple language versions. The iconic nature of the design also lent itself well to incorporation of the character into a series of posters to accompany the videos which were refreshed each month along with the videos.

And finally...

In the last few moments of a movie the story is complete, but we want one last look at the characters in their New World. A glimpse into the happy ever after.

I hope all you marvellous people go away excited, armed with new tools and a new understanding. I hope you take this naming of parts and apply it for all it's worth to make learning drama with real-world impact and every bit as good as TV.

For me, directing drama is a great pleasure, like fronting a band of fantastic session musicians. The technicians, the cast, and the production team, each of whom brings something unique to the party, all come together to sing from the same song sheet – the script. And if the script is a good one, we're laughing. I wish you similar joy in your drama for learning journey.

Thanks

Writing a book is quite an undertaking, one which I wouldn't have been able to complete without the support and assistance of friends and colleagues. So, I would like to express my thanks to:

James Cory-Wright – for sub editing; Melanie Hickmore and Georgia Rooney for text review and feedback; Anita Sullivan for her notes on interactive; Sam Pearce who did the design, typesetting and layout; Jonathan Swain for his beautiful diagrams; Charlotte Schüler, who pointed me at some of the best research; Julian Stodd and David Pearl for publishing advice; Hayley Maisey for her grammatical chops; Monica Amey-Hills for picture research; Carl Thompson for help on image licencing; Paul Van Buuren for the Kuleshov collage and Donald Clark for his moral support.

And my deepest thanks to all the great clients who have trusted me enough to let me practice my craft and to all the amazing actors, technicians, writers and production staff I've had the pleasure and privilege to work with.

© jannoon028 (www.freepik.com) / Final image – Tom Hickmore

Lightning Source UK Ltd.
Milton Keynes UK
UKHW020005280921
391277UK00002B/202